Table of Contents

Amazing Southern Recipes You Will Love

Southern Recipes That Will Satisfy Your Cravings

BY: Ida Smith

License Notes

Introduction

If you are a foodie and love to explore various food ideas, you have come to the right place because there are various amazing recipes here for you to try. What's more interesting is the fact that the recipes are from the south, you know what that means? It simply means that the recipes here are irresistible as southerners know how to cook as well as loving how to cook. At the end of this cookbook, you will discover that every southern recipe here is a must try for you.

Rosemary and Mixed Roasted Potatoes

This is a delectable combination of two different types of potatoes. It gives you a very different taste from what you already know.

Cooking Time: 1 hour 10 minutes

Yield: 5

Ingredient List:

- 1 pound of gold Yukon potatoes, peeled and chopped
- 1/2 pound of red potatoes, peeled and chopped
- 4 tablespoons of oil
- 3 cloves of garlic
- 3 sprigs of fresh rosemary
- 1 teaspoon of salt
- 1/2 tablespoon of ground black pepper.

Preparation:

Heat up your oven to about 400°. Spread your potatoes on a large baking sheet, pour your oil, rosemary, garlic, salt, and pepper to taste on it and mix well. Roast your potatoes 45 minutes and continue turning so all sides can be well roasted.

When your potatoes are soft, remove, and serve while sizzling.

Glazed Salmon in Maple Syrup

Another one of the southern love meals of fresh seafood. It is rich and gives a sweet and sour taste.

Cooking Time: 35 minutes

Yield: 4

Ingredient List:

- 8 ounces of salmon fillets
- 2 tablespoons of oil
- 1/2 teaspoon of black pepper, ground
- 1 teaspoon of salt
- 1/2 cup of melted butter
- 4 tablespoons of maple syrup
- 1 tablespoon of vinegar
- 1 teaspoon of Worcestershire sauce

- 1/2 teaspoon of mustard powder

Preparation:

Sprinkle your salt and pepper over your salmon to taste. Rub each fish with oil and set aside.

Mix your vinegar, syrup, sauce, mustard powder, butter, and pepper together in a bowl and set aside.

Grease your grilling grate, heat up your grill, place your salmon on the great, co et and let it grill for 5 minutes. Open grill and brush your sauce mixture on the fish generously, turn it over and grill for another 10 minutes.

When you are sure your fish is well cooked and crispy, remove from grill and serve while sizzling. You can use crispy chips to serve.

South Style Fried Chicken and Egg

Almost everyone love to have a taste of well fried and crispy chicken; however, you need to move away from your usual and try out the south style fried chicken.

Cooking Time: 40 minutes

Yield: 5

Ingredient List:

- 4 big eggs
- 2 cups of flour
- 1 teaspoon of salt
- 1 teaspoon of black ground pepper
- 4 pounds of chicken, washed, dried, and divided into 10 pieces
- 2 tablespoons of vegetable shortening

Preparation:

First, whisk your eggs in a bowl and add water and mix together. Mix your flour and black pepper in another bowl, season your chicken with salt and pepper, dip it into the egg mixture, dip in the flour mixture to coat and set aside.

Heat your vegetable shortening until it dissolves, add your chicken and simmer until it becomes crispy and brown.

Lastly, remove from heat and serve.

Southern Red Rice

Probably you've not heard about red rice, well you need to give it a try because it is delicious, and your family will love it.

Cooking Time: 60 minutes

Yield: 5

Ingredient List:

- 4 tablespoons of butter
- 1 cup of well diced yellow onions
- 1 cup of well diced green pepper
- 1/2 cup of smoked sausage
- 1 cup of long grain rice
- 1 can of chopped tomatoes
- 1 cup of chicken broth

- 1/2 tablespoon of hot sauce
- 1/2 teaspoon of salt
- 1/2 teaspoon of black pepper

Preparation:

Heat up your oven to about 350°. Then, grease your baking pan with a little butter and set aside.

Dissolve your butter in a pan, add your onions, green pepper, and smoked sausage, cook until it becomes tender, add your rice, tomatoes, hot sauce, broth, salt, and pepper, and let it simmer for about 10 minutes when the sauce begins to thicken.

Transfer to your baking pan, cover with foil, and bake for about 40 minutes when the rice is tender and serve while hot.

Pasta and Cream

There is a saying that it goes the creamier, the better. Our favorite southern pasta and cream is not only quick to prepare but also tastes great, and your kids will love it.

Cooking Time: 30 minutes

Yield: 5

Ingredient List:

- 8 ounces of pasta
- 4 tablespoons of butter
- 2 big eggs
- 1 teaspoon of salt
- 1/2 teaspoon of pepper
- 1/2 teaspoon of mustard powder
- 1 cup of heavy cream

- 1 cup of cheese
- 6 slices of American cheese

Preparation:

First, boil your pasta in a pot of boiling water, drain, and return back to the pot. Add your butter and stir until your butter melts.

Whisk your eggs in a bowl, add your heavy cream, salt, mustard, and pepper. Whisk together and pour the mixture into your pot of pasta. Stir properly.

Lastly, add your cheese, keep stirring until your pasta chickens and becomes very creamy, let it cook for extra 3 minutes and serve while hot.

Piggies and Bacon in a Blanket

This is one appetizer that southerners don't miss out on, and the way it is wrapped makes it more delicious.

Cooking Time: 30 minutes

Yield: 8

Ingredient List:

- 8 pieces of bacon slices
- 1 tablespoon of oil
- 1 pack of crescent rolls
- 16 pieces of cocktail Weiner's
- 1/2 cup of ketchup
- 1 tablespoon of Dijon mustard

Preparation:

Preheat your oven to about 360°. Grease your baking sheet with a little oil.

Cook your bacon in a large pan until it becomes tender, remove from the pan, and cut into two.

Separate the bacon. Cut your rolls into 16 dough, then wrap each bacon with your Weiner.

Place your wrapped bacon on each dough and place in your baking dish. Put in your oven and let it bake for about 15 to 20 minutes or until it becomes golden brown.

Mix your ketchup together with your mustard and serve alongside your baked dough.

Coconut Flavored Potato Ball

You must have been having your sweet potatoes in a different way, and I bet you will want to try out this southern potato dish that leaves you craving for more.

Cooking Time: 1 hour 30 minutes

Yield: 6

Ingredient List:

- 3 pounds of sweet potatoes, peeled, washed, and sliced
- 1/2 cup of brown sugar
- 2 tablespoon of orange juice
- 1 teaspoon of nutmeg powder
- 2 cups of sweetened coconut, shredded
- 2 tablespoons of granulated sugar
- 1 teaspoon of cinnamon powder

- 7 big marshmallows

Preparation:

Heat up your oven to about 360°. Place your potatoes into your baking pan, put in the oven and bake for about 1 hour or until they are tender. Remove your potato and set aside.

Place your potato in a bowl, mash properly, add your brown sugar, nutmeg, and orange juice, stir properly, and set aside.

In another bowl, mix your coconut, cinnamon, and granulated sugar together. Create 6 balls with your potato mixture and marshmallow, roll the balls into your coconut mixture, place in your baking pan and bake for about 20 minutes when your ball begins to bubble and becomes brown.

When it is ready, remove from oven. Serve.

Biscuits and Ham

Anywhere you visit in the south, biscuits and ham go together. Try your hands on this, and you will be glad.

Cooking Time: 25 minutes

Yield: 10

Ingredient List:

- 2 1/2 cups of flour
- 2 tablespoons of sugar
- 1/3 cup of heavy cream
- 1 pound of well chopped cooked ham
- 1/2 cup of butter

Preparation:

Preheat your oven to about 450°. Then, grease your baking sheet with a little butter. Mix your flour and sugar in a bowl, add your heavy cream, and mix properly until it becomes a smooth dough.

Sprinkle flour on a smooth surface and place the dough on it. Gently knead your dough using your hands. Then, use a rolling pin and make it flat but thick.

Get your biscuit cutter, place in flour first, then on your dough then cut out your biscuits.

Place in the baking sheet and bake in your oven for 15 minutes, bring it out and allow it to cool.

Place your butter and harm in a blender, and blend until properly mixed, divide your biscuits into two, add your ham into it and serve while warm.

Turkey Vegetable

You need to try this recipe because you will confess that you haven't tasted any turkey good like this. It is heavenly tasty.

Cooking Time: 60 minutes

Yield: 4

Ingredient List:

- 3 cups of chicken broth
- 1 pounds of smoked turkey wings
- 1 cup of melted butter
- 1 tablespoon of salt
- 1/2 teaspoon of sugar
- 1/2 pound of turnip green, washed, remove the stems, and chop the leaves
- 2 big chopped turnips

Preparation:

Pour your broth into a pot, add your turkey and boil over medium heat. Reduce the heat a little, cook with the pot open for about 20 minutes. Add your butter, sugar, and salt, stir together, then add your green and turnips, stir and let it simmer until your vegetable is tender or for about 30 minutes.

Remove your turkey and vegetables from the heat and serve while hot.

Vegetable Dip and Baked Chips

If you are a lover of the ranch style of dip and dressing, then you will fall in love with this, our unique recipe.

Cooking Time: 10 minutes

Yield: 6

Ingredient List:

- 1/2 teaspoon of ground black pepper
- 1 teaspoon of salt
- 2 teaspoons of lemon juice
- 2 tablespoons of fresh chopped basil leaves
- 2 tablespoons of freshly chopped chives
- 2 tablespoons of well chopped parsley
- 1/2 cup of mayonnaise

- 1/2 cup of buttermilk
- 2 pieces of anchovy
- 1 clove of well chopped garlic
- 1 pack of baked chips

Preparation:

Blend your mayonnaise, buttermilk, parsley, basil, chives, anchovy, garlic, salt, pepper, and lemon juice in a food processor.

Blend until it is very smooth. Then, pour into a bowl and serve with your baked chips.

Baked Yam with Crumbled Pecan

There's no better southern combination than a plate of baked yam and pecan; it comes out crispy and delicious.

Cooking Time: 80 minutes

Yield: 10

Ingredient List:

- 2 cups of cream
- 1/2 teaspoon of cayenne pepper
- 1 big yam, peeled, washed, and cut round
- 1 tablespoon of salt
- 1/2 teaspoon of black pepper ground
- 1/2 teaspoon of thyme
- 2 cups of saline crackers, crushed.

- 1/2 cup of parmesan cheese
- 1/2 cup of pecans, well chopped
- 2 tablespoons of melted butter

Preparation:

Preheat your oven to about 350°. Then, grease your baking pan with a little butter. Set aside.

Mix your cayenne pepper, and cream together in a bowl and set aside.

Arrange part of the yam into your baking pan, season with a little thyme, salt, and black pepper. Pour part of your cream mixture, place another set of yam on top and repeat the process for every layer until you exhaust your yam.

Mix your crackers, pecans, cheese, and butter in another bowl, mix properly and scatter all over your yam casserole. Cover with foil. Then, bake for about 20 minutes. Remove foil and bake again until it becomes golden brown and your yams are soft. Bake for another 40 minutes, remove, and serve while sizzling.

Cooked Shrimp and Vegetables

Cooked shrimp with vegetables is served in the south; it is tasty and has a unique taste. It could be used as a starter even at a party.

Cooking Time: 70 minutes

Yield: 4

Ingredient List:

- 2 cups of oil
- 2 tablespoons of Dijon mustard
- 1/2 cup of white vinegar
- 1/3 cup of mayonnaise
- 1 tablespoon of pickle relish well drained
- 1/2 teaspoon of garlic powder
- 1/3 teaspoon of salt

- 1/3 teaspoon of pepper
- 1 pound of cooked and peeled shrimp
- 1 teaspoon of hot sauce
- 2 cups of lettuce, shredded

Preparation:

Mix your oil, vinegar, mustard, mayonnaise, garlic, salt, hot sauce, pepper, and relish together in a bowl and it in the fridge for 1 hour.

Toss your shrimp into the mixture, combine together, and serve it chilled together with your lettuce as topping.

Tortilla Chips and Crispy Tilapia

Seafood is not only mouthwatering delicious but also very nutritious. This tilapia recipe is a must try for every home.

Cooking Time: 30 minutes

Yield: 4

Ingredient List:

- 1 cup of tortilla chips, crushed
- 1/2 cup of melted butter
- 1 tablespoon of lime zest, grated
- 1/2 teaspoon of dried basil
- 4 ounces of tilapia fillets, skinned
- 1 teaspoon of house seasoning

Preparation:
First, preheat your oven to about 400°. Line your baking pan with foil. Then, set aside.

Mix your crushed chips, basil, zest, and butter In a bowl and set aside.

Place your tilapia fish in the pan, season it with your house seasoning, spread your chips mixture on the fish and bake for about 20 minutes.

Lastly, when the fish is golden brown and crispy, remove from oven and serve sizzling.

Bread and Tomato Sandwich

This might probably sound strange to your ears, but then you are in shock because the taste of our bread and tomato sandwich is quite pleasant to your tongue.

Cooking Time: 15 minutes

Yield: 8

Ingredient List:

- 6 small sized tomatoes
- 8 bread slices
- 1 cup of mayonnaise
- 1 tablespoon of seasoning
- 1/2 cup of chopped parsley

Preparation:

Wash your tomatoes and thinly cut them, then place the slices on a paper towel to drain out any liquid

Using your biscuit cutter, cut some round shape from the bread, spread your mayonnaise on the bread.

Sprinkle your seasoning on your tomato, place each tomato slice on your bread and too with another bread round. Place your parsley on the sandwich and serve.

Spicy Fried Oysters and Sauce

Looking for a special southern love meal to make your loved one happy? Well, this recipe of fried spicy oysters will surely make your lover happy and even ask for more.

Cooking Time: 30 minutes

Yield: 2

Ingredient List:

- 1/2 cup of mayonnaise
- 1/3 teaspoon of well chopped tarragon
- 2 cups of oil
- 1/3 cup of cornmeal, ground
- 1/2 pound of fresh oysters, washed, drained, and dried
- 1 teaspoon of salt
- 1 teaspoon of black pepper

Preparation:

Mix your mayonnaise and tarragon in a bowl and put in the refrigerator.

Heat your oil in a pan. While the oil is heating over medium heat, put your cornmeal in a bowl, sprinkle a little salt and pepper on your oyster to taste, dip into the cornmeal and fry.

You actually need to be careful to avoid oil spilling on you, fry both sides of the oyster until it becomes golden brown. Remove from oil, drain with a paper towel, and serve with your mayonnaise mixture that was reserved in the fridge.

Baked Eggs and Grits

This is an easy to prepare recipe that can be served as breakfast or even light dinner. With a very low budget, you are good to go.

Cooking Time: 20 minutes

Yield: 4

Ingredient List:

- 1/2 teaspoon of black pepper
- 1/2 teaspoon of salt
- 1/2 teaspoon of garlic powder
- 1/2 cup of cooking grits
- 1 cup of cheddar cheese, shredded
- 1/3 cup of chopped ham
- 4 medium sized eggs

- 1 tablespoon of scallions
- 1 tablespoon of oil

Preparation:

Preheat your oven to about 300°. Grease your baking pan with a little oil and set aside.

Cook your grits in a pan according to the direction on the pack. Once it is cooked, add your cheese, ham, salt, pepper, and garlic powder, stir continuously until your cheese melts.

Share the grits mixture into four places in your pan, make a nest in the middle of each, crack your eggs and pour into the nest, garnish with a little salt and pepper, and top with your cheese.

Put in your already heated oven and bake for about 20 minutes when your egg white is firm, but ensure your yolk is still runny, bring it out and serve while hot. Sprinkle your scallion In too and serve.

Creamy Shrimp Pie

You must be very familiar with shrimp; however, you need to try out this delicious shrimp pie and thank me later.

Cooking Time: 55 minutes

Yield: 8

Ingredient List:

- 2 tablespoons of butter
- 2 medium sized yellow onions, well chopped
- 2 medium sized green bell pepper, well diced
- 1 teaspoon of salt
- 4 cups of peeled, cooked, and deveined shrimp
- 2 cups of bread crumbs, fresh
- 2 cups of milk

- 2 big eggs
- 1/2 teaspoon of black pepper
- 4 slices of chopped bacon

Preparation:

Heat up your oven to about 300°. Grease your baking pan lightly and set aside.

Heat your butter in a large pan, add your green pepper, onions, a little salt, stir together and let it simmer until your vegetables are soft.

Lay your shrimp in your baking pan, add your crumbs, and vegetable mixture. Whisk your eggs, a little salt, black pepper, and milk in a small bowl and pour the mixture into the pan.

Lay your bacon on top the mixture and bake for about 40 minutes, when it is set and crispy, remove from baking pan.

Cut into 8 pie size and serve.

Baked Cheesy Macaroni

This is one recipe that you will be proud to serve; it is very rich and creamy, and your family will love it.

Cooking Time: 60 minutes

Yield: 5

Ingredient List:

- 8 ounces of macaroni
- 2 cups of shredded cheese
- 4 tablespoons of butter
- 3 large sized eggs
- 1 cup of milk
- 4 tablespoons of sour cream
- 1 teaspoon of salt

Preparation:

Preheat your oven to about 360°. Grease your baking pan with a little butter and set aside.

Boil your macaroni in a pot of salty boiling water following the direction on the pack. When it us tender, drain the water and set aside in a bowl.

Add your cheese, reserving a little, and your butter into your cooked macaroni and stir properly until your macaroni is well coated.

Whisk your eggs in a bowl, add your milk, sour cream, and salt. Stir properly and add the mixture into your pasta, stir properly and transfer to your baking pan.

Bake for about 40 minutes or until it becomes golden brown, bring it out and too with your reserved cheese and bake for extra 5 minutes or until your cheese melts, bring it out and serve while sizzling.

Creamy Chicken

The creamy chicken can be served with any side meal of your choice, or you can decide to take it like that while watching a movie or having a little family time.

Cooking Time: 25 minutes

Yield: 4

Ingredient List:

- 2 tablespoons of butter
- 1 tablespoon of flour
- 2 cups of chicken breast cooked and chopped.
- 1/3 cup of chicken broth
- 1/2 cup of half and half
- 2 teaspoons of sherry, dried
- 1/3 tablespoon of dried thyme

- 1 teaspoon of salt
- 1 teaspoon of black ground pepper
- 1 tablespoon of chopped parsley

Preparation:
Heat your butter in a pan. Add your flour to it and heat, while continuously stirring until it begins to bubble. Add your broth, sherry, and half and half, allow it to boil while you continue to stir. Stir until it becomes thick and creamy.

Add your chicken, thyme, pepper, and salt heat a little and serve. Garnish with your parsley.

Noodles and Beef

Southern noodles are special and are served with either beef or chicken to go with.

Cooking Time: 70 minutes

Yield: 4

Ingredient List:

- 10 ounces of noodles
- 2 tablespoons of oil
- 2 small sized yellow onions, well diced
- 1 clove of well diced garlic
- 1 pound of ground beef
- 1/2 teaspoon of salt
- 1/3 teaspoon of ground black pepper
- 1 can of pasta sauce

- 1/2 cup of cheese
- 1 pound of chopped mozzarella cheese
- 1 cup of parmesan, grated

Preparation:

Preheat your oven to about 360°. Grease your baking pan with butter and set aside.

Boil your noodles according to the direction on the pack, drain and set aside.

Heat up your frying pan, heat your oil, add your onions and fry for about 5 minutes, add your garlic and cook for another 1 minutes. Add your beef and cook for about 7 minutes.

Add your salt and pepper to it, add your sauce, cheese, and still continuously until your cheese melts. Spoon part of the beef sauce onto your baking pan, top with your noodles, add your sauce, mozzarella, and parmesan preserving a little mozzarella and parmesan. Repeat the same layering prices until you have used up your ingredients.

Cover it with your foil and bake for about 30 minutes. Remove your foil and continue baking for an extra 20 minutes. Bring it out and serve hit.

Baked Pineapple Flavored Chicken

Having a combination of pineapple and chicken gives you a sweet and salty taste, and it tastes unique and delicious.

Cooking Time: 60 minutes

Yield: 4

Ingredient List:

- 2 tablespoons of oil
- 2 pounds of chicken legs
- 1 teaspoon of salt
- 1/2 teaspoon of black ground pepper
- 2 cans of crushed and drained pineapple
- 2 teaspoons of hot sauce
- 1 cup of ritz, crushed

- 1/2 cup of melted butter
- 1 cup of cheddar cheese, grated

Preparation:

Heat up your oven to about 360°. Then, grease your baking dish with a little butter and set aside.

Next, heat your oil in a large pan, season your chicken with a little salt and black pepper, place in your heated oil, and let it simmer, turning both sides until it becomes brown or for 10 minutes. Then, remove from oil, place on a paper towel, and drain.

Mix your pineapple and got sauce in a bowl and spread the mixture in your baking dish, place the chicken on top. Mix your ritz, cheese, and butter in another bowl and sprinkle the mixture over your chicken.

Lastly, put in the oven and bake for about 45 minutes or until your chicken is well cooked. Take it to your table straight with the baking pan and serve there while sizzling.

Ravioli and Pecan

This savory southern dish will leave a lasting sweet and salty taste in your mouth. Having squash with ravioli is also a great idea.

Cooking Time: 30 minutes

Yield: 5

Ingredient List:

- 1 pound of ravioli
- 4 tablespoons of butter
- 1/2 cup of well chopped pecan
- 1/2 teaspoon of salt
- 1/2 teaspoon of ground black pepper

Preparation:

Boil your ravioli in a pot of boiling salt water when it is tender, drain and set aside.

Melt your butter in a heated pan, and your pecans and cook while stirring continuously. Cook until your pecan becomes brown, add your ravioli, pepper, and salt, cook for about 2 minutes, and stir until your ravioli is well coated, then serve while hot.

Baked Spicy Meat Loaf

Meat loaf has always been a nice dessert to serve to kids and family; try our unique recipe and come back for more.

Cooking Time: 1 hour 20 minutes
Yield: 8
Ingredient List:

- 2 pounds of ground beef
- 1 cup of chopped yellow onions
- 1 cup of chopped green pepper
- 1 big egg, whisked
- 1 can of diced tomatoes
- 1 cup of cooking oat
- 1/2 teaspoon of black pepper

- 1 tablespoon of salt
- 2 tablespoons of ketchup
- 2 tablespoons of brown sugar
- 1 tablespoon of ground yellow mustard

Preparation:

Heat up your oven to about 350°. Mix your beef, green pepper, onion, egg, tomatoes, oat, black pepper, and salt together in a bowl, use your hands to mix properly and pour the mixture into your baking dish and shape it into the form of meat loaf.

Mix your ketchup, mustard, and brown sugar in a bowl, spread the mixture on your meat loaf and bake for about 1 hour or until it becomes tender and brown.

Remove from oven and serve while hot.

Spicy Shrimp with Cajun Seasoning

You obviously cannot get enough of this southern dish because serving your shrimp got spiciness that will leave you begging for more.

Cooking Time: 20 minutes

Yield: 4

Ingredient List:

- 2 tablespoons of oil
- 4 tablespoons of butter
- 1 pound of large sized peeled shrimp
- 1 tablespoon of Cajun seasoning
- 10 ounces of linguine
- 1 tablespoon of diced garlic
- 1/2 cup of chicken broth

- 1 tablespoon of hot sauce
- 1 cup of scallions
- 1/2 cup of parmesan cheese, grated

Preparation:

First, in a large pan, heat up your oil. Add part of your butter and let it heat. Dip your shrimp into your Cajun seasoning and put it in the pan, let it shimmer then turn the other side also and let it shimmer for 3 minutes, then transfer to a bowl and set aside.

Boil your linguine in a pot of boiling water until it is tender and drain. While cooking your linguine, dissolve your left over butter in a pan, add garlic and simmer for 1 minute.

Then, add your broth to the pan and hot sauce and let it simmer. Turn off the fire and return your shrimp to the pan.

Mix your linguine together with your shrimp sauce and sprinkle your scallion on top and serve while hot. Serve with your parmesan cheese.

Seasoned Cabbage and Corned Beef

Looking for a quick southern meal to prepare for your little family get together? You can never go wrong with this meal.

Cooking Time: 30 minutes

Yield: 6

Ingredient List:

- 2 pounds of corned beef
- 1 big head of cabbage
- 1/2 cup of butter
- 1 tablespoon of house seasoning
- 3 cups of water

Preparation:

Place your corned beef in a pot, put enough water in it and let it boil. Reduce the heat, cover the pot, and let it simmer until your beef is tender. Remove the beef and set aside.

Chop your cabbage and separate the dark green side from the light green, chop it and set aside. Place the light green part of the cabbage in a bowl and rinse properly.

Melt your butter in a pan and add your cabbage to it, stir properly until your cabbage is coated with the butter. Add your house seasoning, cover the pot, and let it simmer until your cabbage is soft and crispy.

Remove from pot, place in your serving plate, slice your corned beef and place on the cabbage and serve.

South Smoky Spaghetti

This recipe can be considered as everything in one together with a flavor that gives it a unique taste.

Cooking Time: 30 minutes

Yield: 6

Ingredient List:

- 1 pound of chopped bacon
- 1/2 cup of hot sauce
- 1/2 cup of parmesan cheese, grated
- 1/2 cup of heavy cream
- 1 teaspoon of ground black pepper
- 2 medium sized eggs
- 1 medium sized onion, well chopped
- 1 teaspoon of salt

- 1 pack of spaghetti

Preparation:

First, cook your bacon in a large pan, until it becomes crispy. Drain and dry using a paper towel and set aside.

Whisk your eggs, cream, parmesan, a little salt, part of your hot sauce, and pepper together in a bowl. Then boil your spaghetti in a pot of already boiling water and add salt to it. When it is well cooked drain and set aside.

Then, return your pan to heat, add your onions and simmer for 5 minutes. Remove the pan from the heat. Add your spaghetti, bacon, and egg mixture to the pan, stir well until it becomes creamy.

Add a little more got sauce and salt mix properly and serve hot.

Well Seasoned Rib Roast and Fried Potato

There's nothing as good as having good roasted meat to chew on while waiting for dinner or watching a movie with your family.

Cooking Time: 1 hour 30 minutes

Yield: 4

Ingredient List:

- 5 pounds of standing rib roast
- 1 tablespoon of house seasoning
- 2 cups of fried potato chips

Preparation:

Keep your rib roast to stand for about 1 hour. Heat up your oven to about 360°. Place your rack in a roasting pan.

Rub your rib roast together with your seasoning and place on your roasting rack with the fatty side faced up and let it roast for about 1 hour.

Leave the roast in the oven until you are ready to serve. Grill the roast again until it is well roasted and serve while sizzling together with your potato.

Smoked Turkey and Rice

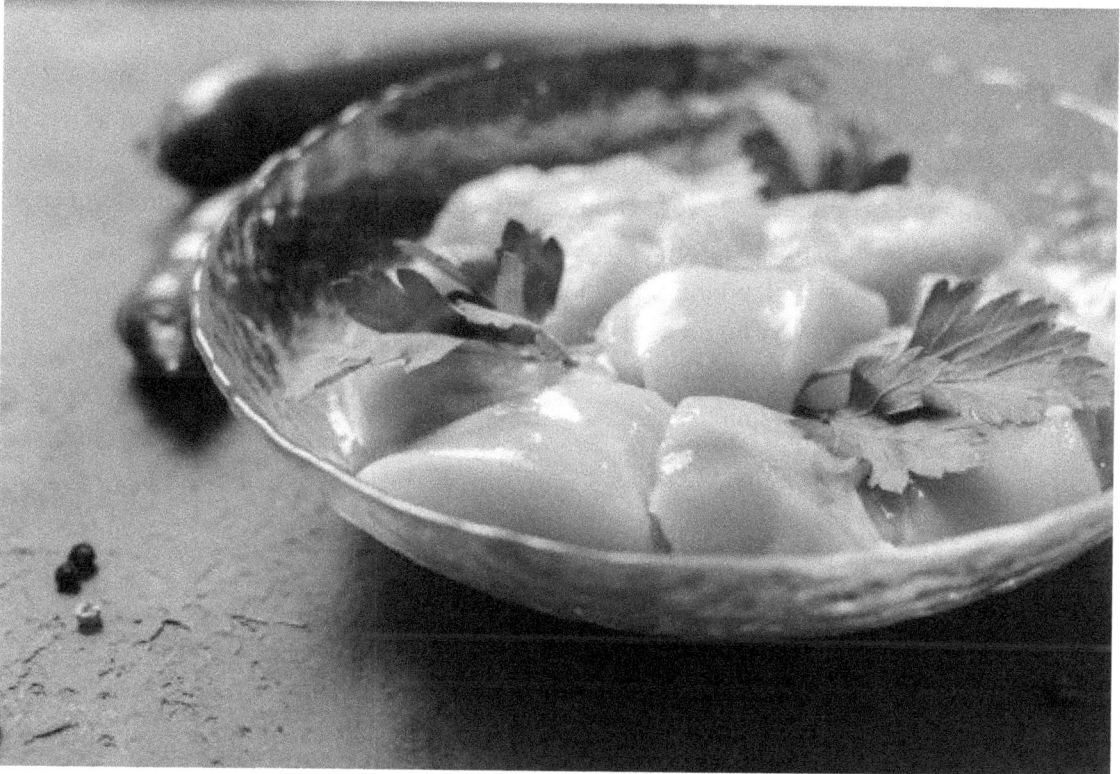

Southerners love rice, and they also grow rice; hence, they have various ways of cooking their rice. Here is another unique dish of rice.

Cooking Time: 50 minutes

Yield: 4

Ingredient List:

- 2 tablespoons of butter
- 2 slices of well chopped bacon
- 1/2 cup of diced yellow onion
- 1 clove of well chopped garlic
- 6 ounces of well cut turkey
- 2 cups of white long grain rice
- 1/2 cup of well diced tomato

- 10 ounces of smoked turkey wings
- 1 teaspoon of salt
- 1 teaspoon of black pepper
- 2 tablespoons of chopped scallion

Preparation:

Heat up your oven to about 360°. Melt your butter in a pan. Then, add your bacon and cook for about 5 minutes or until it becomes crispy. Add your onions and cook until it is tender. Then add your garlic and cook for another minute, add your chopped turkey, cook for an extra 2 minutes, add your rice, tomato, smoked turkey wings, pepper, and salt to taste

Add water and allow it to boil, pour it into your baking pan and bake for about 30 minutes or until your rice becomes tender and every liquid absorbed.

Remove from oven and serve while hot.

Leftover Rice Cakes

In the south, their love for food is overwhelming, and even their leftover rice is used to make delicious rice cakes.

Cooking Time: 30 minutes

Yield: 10

Ingredient List:

- 2 cups of already cooked leftover rice
- 1 teaspoon of salt
- 1 teaspoon of black pepper
- 1 big egg, cracked and whisked
- 1 cup of parmesan cheese, grated
- 1/2 cup of bread crumbs, dried
- 1 cup of oil
- 1 tablespoon of onion powder

Preparation:

Toss your rice in a bowl, add your salt and pepper to taste, add your whisked egg, onion, and parmesan. Mix properly with your hands.

Next, take a little rice mixture, put in your palms and squeeze. Then, give it the shape you want, dip in your bread crumb, and set aside. Do same until your rice mixture is exhausted.

Then, heat your oil in a large pan over medium heat. Put in your rice cakes and fry until it becomes brown. Turn the other side and fry for about 5 minutes.

Drain on a paper towel and serve when warm.

Mushroom and Brown Rice from the South

This is another way southerners make their rice; it is tasty, and your family will love it.

Cooking Time: 30 minutes

Yield: 4

Ingredient List:

- 4 tablespoons of butter
- 2 medium sized yellow onions, well diced
- 1 cup of white long grain rice
- 1 can of mushrooms, drained and sliced
- 2 cups of beef broth
- 1/2 teaspoon of salt
- 1/2 cup of chopped parsley

Preparation:

First, heat up your butter in a pan. Then, add your onions and cook for about 10 minutes or until it becomes tender and golden brown.

Add your rice, and mushrooms to the pan, stir properly and cook for about 2 minutes. Add your broth, and salt and boil properly, reduce the heat, cover your pot, and cook under low heat until your liquid is absorbed and your rice is soft.

Lastly, remove from heat, set aside for about 5 minutes, and serve topped with your parsley.

Conclusion

Now you have 30 unique and mouthwatering recipes from the south that you can always try. They are easy to prepare and taste delicious. Making any of our recipes with your loved ones will make them come back for more.

Don't miss out!

Visit the website below and you can sign up to receive emails whenever Ida Smith publishes a new book. There's no charge and no obligation.

https://books2read.com/r/B-A-LRXL-YVVJB

BOOKS 2 READ

Connecting independent readers to independent writers.

www.ingramcontent.com/pod-product-compliance
Lightning Source LLC
Chambersburg PA
CBHW081300040426
42452CB00014B/2588